How We Use

Silk

Carol Ballard

Raintree

www.raintreepublishers.co.uk
Visit our website to find out more information about **Raintree** books.

To order:
☎ Phone 44 (0) 1865 888112
📄 Send a fax to 44 (0) 1865 314091
💻 Visit the Raintree bookshop at **www.raintreepublishers.co.uk** to browse our catalogue and order online.

First published in Great Britain by Raintree, Halley Court, Jordan Hill, Oxford OX2 8EJ, part of Harcourt Education.
Raintree is a registered trademark of Harcourt Education Ltd.

Editorial: Nick Hunter and Richard Woodham
Design: Kim Saar and Bridge Creative Services Ltd
Picture Research: Maria Joannou and Debra Weatherley
Production: Amanda Meaden
Indexing: Indexing Specialists (UK) Ltd

Originated by Ambassador Litho Ltd
Printed and bound in Hong Kong, China by South China Printing Company

ISBN 1 844 43439 7
09 08 07 06 05
10 9 8 7 6 5 4 3 2 1

British Library Cataloguing in Publication Data
Ballard, Carol
How We Use Silk. – (Using Materials)
677.3'9
A full catalogue record for this book is available from the British Library.

Acknowledgements
The publishers would like to thank the following for permission to reproduce photographs: Associated Press p. **21**; Bridgeman Art Library p. **26**; Corbis pp. **5** (Christie's Images), **14** (Harcourt Index), **15** (Lawrence Manning), **16** (Dave Houser), **17** (Kevin Morris), **19** (Macduff Everton), **20** (Peter Turnley), **27**; Getty Images pp. **13**, **23** (Imagebank), **24** (Photodisc), **25** (Photodisc), **28** (Photodisc/Harcourt Index); Naturepl p. **7** (top) (Pete Oxford); Oxford Scientific Films pp. **8**, **18** (Deni Brown), **29** (Michael Fogden); photos12.com p. **12**; Powerstock p. **22**; Science Photo Library pp. **4** (R.E Lichfield), **6** (Pascal Goetgheluck), **7** (bott) (Pascal Goetgheluck), **9** (Pascal Goetgheluck), **10** (Pascal Goetgheluck), **11** (Eye of Science).

Cover photograph of bolts of colourful silk for sale in a Korean market, reproduced with permission of Corbis.

Every effort has been made to contact copyright holders of any material reproduced in this book. Any omissions will be rectified in subsequent printings if notice is given to the publishers.

The paper used to print this book comes from sustainable resources.

Contents

Any words appearing in bold, **like this**, are explained in the Glossary.

Silk and its properties

All the things we use are made from materials. Silk is a material. Silk threads can be spun and woven to make a very soft **fabric**. This fabric has been used for hundreds of years to make beautiful clothes and many other things.

This silk fabric has been magnified thousands of times by a **microscope**.

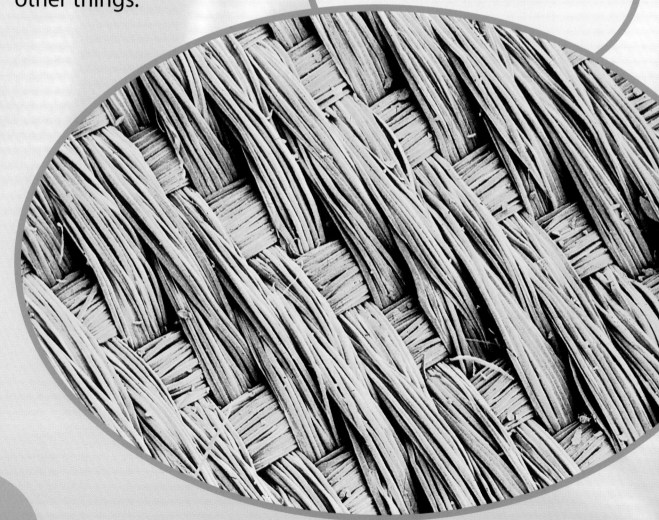

This beautiful old silk robe once belonged to a very wealthy family.

The **properties** of a material tell us what it is like. Silk has some very special properties. It is strong, light, soft and shiny. These properties mean silk has lots of uses. Scientists can make **synthetic** fibres that have many of the same properties as silk. These are much cheaper than silk. Many people still prefer real silk, though, especially for **luxury** clothes.

Don't use it!

*The different properties of materials make them useful for some jobs. These properties also make them unsuitable for other jobs. For example, we do not normally use silk for making raincoats. Silk is not **waterproof**.*

Where does silk come from?

Silk is a **natural** material. It is made by animals called silkworms. Most silk comes from silkworms kept on farms, but some still comes from wild silkworms. Fine threads and cloth can be made from the silk that animals produce.

A silkworm is actually a caterpillar, not a worm. It will turn into a moth when it is an adult.

This silk farmer is collecting silkworm cocoons.

Silkworms grow best if they have fresh **mulberry** leaves to eat, so it is easiest to produce silk in areas where mulberry trees grow well. Most of the silk farms in the world are in China, although there are many in countries such as Japan, India, Korea and the USA. Some silk farms are small and have just a few workers. Others are huge and employ many people.

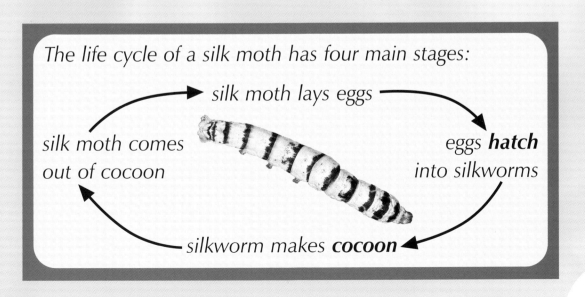

The life cycle of a silk moth has four main stages:

silk moth lays eggs

*eggs **hatch** into silkworms*

*silkworm makes **cocoon***

silk moth comes out of cocoon

How do silkworms make silk?

Eggs laid by female silk moths are collected by the farmer. They are put into an **incubator** until they **hatch**. After hatching, the tiny silkworms are moved to feeding trays. The silkworms grow quickly, feeding on fresh **mulberry** leaves for about a month. Then they are put on to wooden racks. Each spins a special silk case around itself. It is called a **cocoon**.

This female silk moth will lay about 500 eggs.

Silkworms
are very greedy!

A silkworm makes the
silk thread inside its body.
It spins the silk out
through two tiny tubes
called **spinnerets**, near
its mouth. As it spins it
moves its head in a figure
of eight pattern. The silk
thread is soft and sticky
at first but soon hardens
in the air. The silkworm
takes about three days to
make the cocoon.

Silkworm facts and figures

*Silkworms do not drink.
They get all the water
they need from the leaves
they eat. In the month
between hatching and
making its cocoon, a
silkworm will eat nearly
30,000 times its own
weight of mulberry leaves!
It grows so quickly that it
sheds its skin four times.*

Processing silk

The finished **cocoons** are taken from the wooden racks by the silk farmer and soaked in hot water to loosen the strands of silk, called **filaments**. Slowly, the cocoons are unwound. Filaments from several cocoons are twisted together and spun to make a strong thread. Not all the silk from a cocoon is twisted and spun into high-quality thread. Loose ends and tangled threads are used to make poorer-quality thread.

These cocoons are being unwound. The silk filaments are being twisted and spun into a strong thread.

Here you can see how several filaments are twisted together to make a single silk thread.

The threads are boiled in soapy water to remove the sticky gum that coats each thread. Without the gum, the silk is much lighter. The silk can be made heavier again by soaking it in special **chemicals**. Silk that is not soaked in these chemicals is called pure silk.

How thick?

*Silk threads can be spun to make fibres of different thicknesses. The threads are measured in units called **deniers** – the larger the denier, the thicker the thread. The thicker threads are used to make thick silk. Very thin threads are needed to make the finest silk cloth.*

Silk in history

Silk has been made in China for thousands of years.
Tiny pieces of silk cloth have been found
in ancient Chinese tombs.

In Europe, merchants like these could get rich by selling silk.

Silk traders

Merchants used to travel thousands of miles to bring silk from China to Europe. They used *mules* to carry the silk which they exchanged in Europe for fruit, cotton and precious metals. The paths they travelled along became known as the Silk Route.

At one time, silk was regarded as so special that only members of the Chinese royal family were allowed to wear it.

The Chinese tried to keep the secret of how to make silk. They sold silk to other countries for a lot of money and precious goods. If other countries had known about silkworms, they would have been able to make their own silk. Chinese silk would then have become less valuable. Giving the secret away was punished by death. But eventually the secret leaked out and silk began to be produced in other countries.

Using silk thread

Some people use silk thread in fine **embroidery**. The stitches look shiny. Mixing silk with ordinary cotton thread makes that shiny, too. Many people use this type of thread for plain sewing. Silk thread can also be used for stitching wounds after operations. It is a good thread to use because it is strong, easy to knot and does not work loose.

Silk used for stitching wounds is unlikely to break before the wound heals.

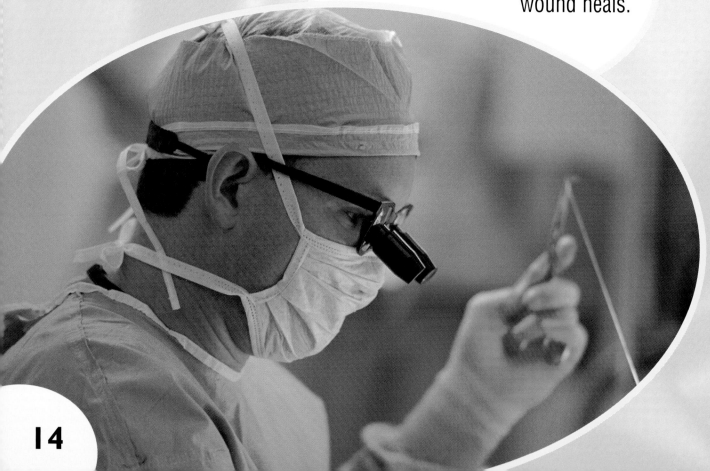

This instrument is called a pipa. The four strings were traditionally made from silk.

Traditional musical instruments from the Far East often had silk strings. Silk strings are also used on more modern instruments such as harps, lutes and mandolins. The silk strings give a soft sound when they are played. Some fishermen use silk in their fishing lines. Silk threads are stronger than many other fibres.

Chinese embroidery

Some of the most beautiful embroidery in the world comes from the Suzhou region of China. It is made using very fine silk thread and tiny needles. Stitches are made very carefully on a thin material that is stretched across a frame. When it is finished the picture looks the same on the back and on the front!

Making silk cloth

Silk threads can be woven together to make silk cloth.
A machine called a **loom** is set up with long threads of
silk running from one end to the other. These are the
warp threads. A **shuttle** is wound with thread and
moved across the warp threads from one side of the loom
to the other. The threads from
the shuttle are called the
weft threads.

A loom can make silk cloth
very quickly.

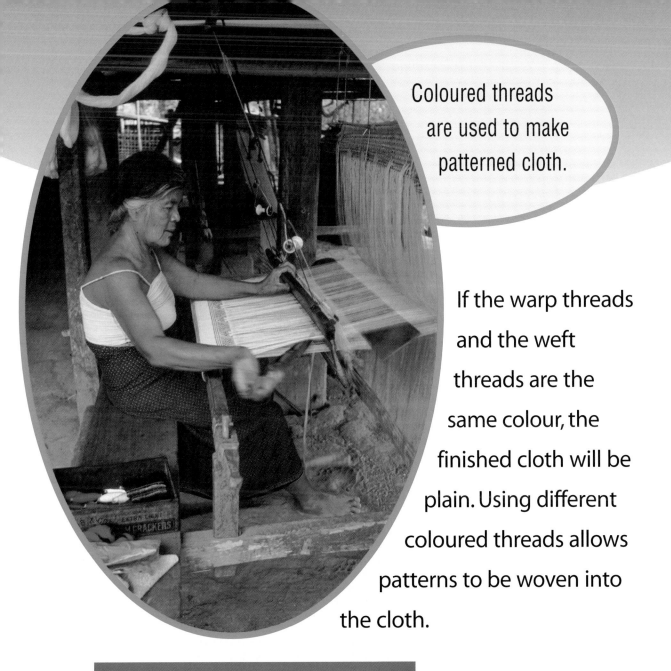

Coloured threads are used to make patterned cloth.

If the warp threads and the weft threads are the same colour, the finished cloth will be plain. Using different coloured threads allows patterns to be woven into the cloth.

Don't use it!

Silk becomes heavy and weak when it gets wet. This means that it is not a good material to use for making things that will be used in water. For example, we don't use silk to make swimming costumes.

Everyday clothes are often made with wool, cotton or man-made **fabrics**. Silk cloth is normally only used for **luxury** clothes.

Coloured silk

Silk from farmed silkworms is white. **Dyes** must be used to colour it. In the past, these dyes were made from plants. Berries, leaves, roots and petals were crushed and their coloured juices were collected.

Silk is **absorbent**. By dipping silk in plant juices, it can be dyed many different colours.

Indigo plants like this were used to make a deep blue dye.

Silk can be dyed to produce a whole rainbow of colours!

Today, man-made dyes are used instead. Huge **vats** are filled with coloured dye and the bundles of silk thread are put in. The threads absorb the dye.

Wild silk

*Wild silkworms spin silk **cocoons** but their silk is not white. Depending on the **species** of silkworm, the silk can be red, pale gold or silvery-grey.*

They then have to be washed to remove any extra dye. Some threads are dyed so that they are the same colour throughout. Others are dyed unevenly, so that there are different shades of colour along their length. These can be used to make beautiful scarves.

Silk for clothes

Clothes made from silk are worn in many different parts of the world. Silk has been used for centuries in India to make traditional clothes such as saris. It is now used to make a wide range of clothing including ties, dresses and scarves.

People in Asia use silk in different colours for special clothes.

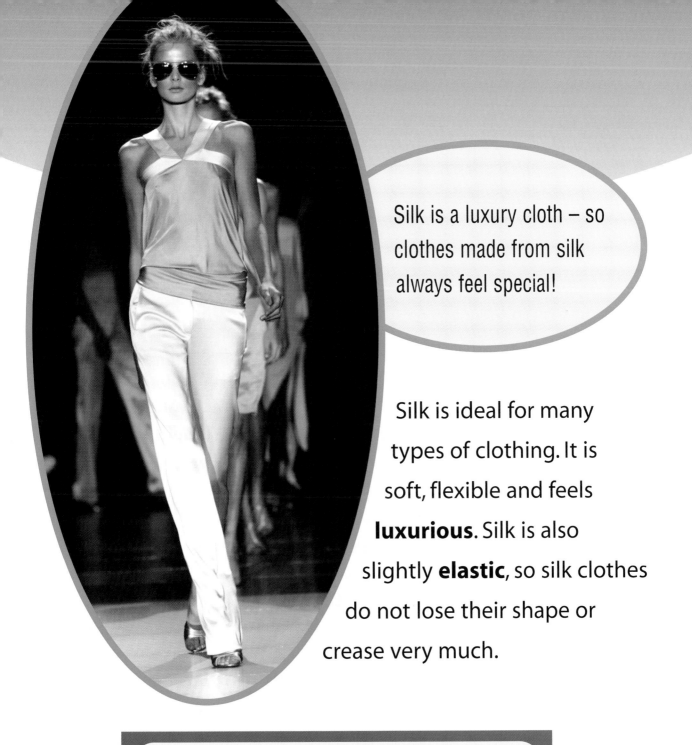

Silk is a luxury cloth – so clothes made from silk always feel special!

Silk is ideal for many types of clothing. It is soft, flexible and feels **luxurious**. Silk is also slightly **elastic**, so silk clothes do not lose their shape or crease very much.

Silk in the heat

*Silk clothes are very comfortable to wear in hot places. This is because silk clothes can **absorb** sweat from your skin but still feel dry. They help you to stay cool.*

Silk for warmth

Heat cannot pass easily through silk. It is a **thermal insulator**. This means that it traps heat around your body, keeping you warm. Clothes made from silk feel much warmer than clothes of the same thickness made from **fabrics** such as linen or cotton.

This mountaineer wears thin silk gloves inside his thick outer gloves to help him stay warm.

A silk-lined sleeping bag can keep you warm in the coldest places.

Wearing a thin layer of silk underneath your outer clothes is a good way to stay warm. Silk gloves, socks and underwear can all help to keep you warm on a cold day. Some people like to sleep in silk pyjamas or nightdresses.

Many campers use a sleeping bag at night. Even after a warm, sunny day it can be cold at night. Some people put a silk lining inside their sleeping bag to trap all their body heat and keep themselves as warm as possible.

Don't use it!
*Silk is warm and cosy but it is very expensive. Materials like wool and some **synthetic** fibres are much cheaper and easier to produce. These can keep us just as warm so we normally use them instead of silk.*

Silk-screen printing

Silk-screen printing is also called serigraphy. It can be used to make beautiful pictures. It can also be used for putting designs on to **fabrics** such as cotton T-shirts. Silk cloth is used because it is very fine. Designs stay crisp and clear.

This picture has been printed using the silk-screen method.

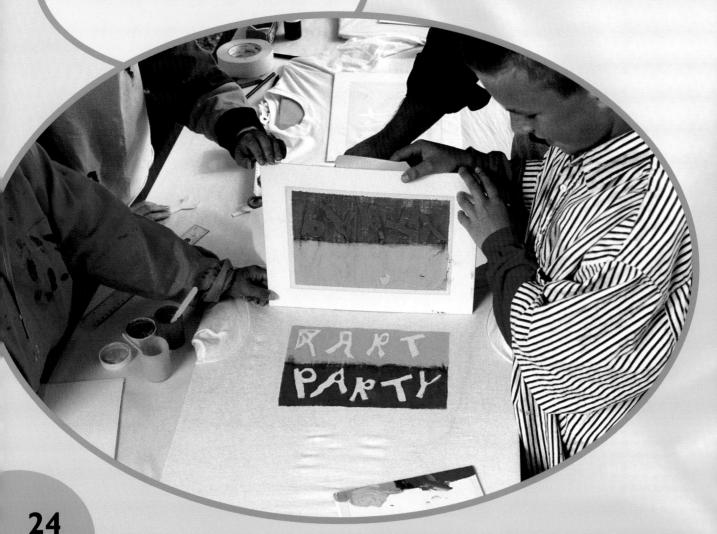

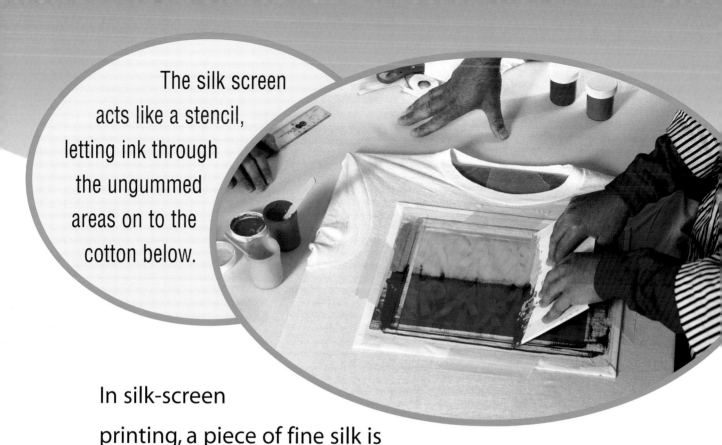

The silk screen acts like a stencil, letting ink through the ungummed areas on to the cotton below.

In silk-screen printing, a piece of fine silk is stretched over a frame. The design is then drawn on to the silk. Gum is spread over parts of the silk to stop ink getting through. The frame is laid on top of a piece of material. Ink or paint is poured on to the silk and spread over the whole surface using a special tool. Only the ungummed areas let ink through. The frame is carefully removed and the ink and gum are cleaned off the silk.

Multi-coloured printing

For designs that need more than one colour, the same process is used. After the first printing, gum is spread over different areas of the silk. The material is then printed on to again using another colour.

Other uses of silk

Silk is beautiful, strong, **elastic**, soft and light. These **properties** mean it can be used for many different things. Silk **fabric** can be used for decorations. Some artists use special paints to make pictures on silk. Coloured silk is also used to make beautiful **artificial** flowers.

An artist painted this picture on silk instead of paper.

Parachutes like this used to be made of silk.

Some special types of clothes are made of silk. Racehorse jockeys need to be as light as possible. They also need to keep warm. They wear bright silk shirts. Clothes worn on special occasions, such as wedding dresses and veils, are often made of silk because it is **luxurious**.

Don't use it!

*Silk was used to make the first parachutes. Making them from silk was very expensive as they are made from a huge amount of material. We don't make parachutes from silk today. Cheaper, **synthetic** materials such as nylon have been developed that are just as strong and light.*

Silk and the environment

A spider spins its web with silk from **spinnerets** at the end of its body.

Silk is a **natural** fibre. This means that it will decay and the **chemicals** that it is made from will be released back into the ground. This is good for the **environment**. Some man-made fibres such as nylon and rayon are used as alternatives to silk but these decay very slowly. They are not good for the environment.

Silk from spiders

Spiders spin a type of silk to make their webs. It is very strong and can be woven into clothes. In 1896, Queen Victoria was given a spider-silk gown by the Chinese.

28

Using wild silk
moths like this one may be a good
way to produce coloured silk.

Some of the chemical **dyes** that are used to colour silk
are not good for the environment. Natural plant dyes are
rarely used because they do not give such good results.
A new idea is to use wild silkworms that make coloured
silks. By breeding them carefully, different coloured silks
could be produced instead of just white silks.

Find out for yourself

The best way to find out more about silk is to investigate it for yourself. Look around your home for things made from silk, and keep an eye out for silk during your day. Think about why silk was used for each job. What properties make it suitable? You will find the answers to many of your questions in this book. You can also look in other books and on the Internet.

Books to read

Science Answers: Grouping Materials, Carol Ballard (Heinemann Library, 2003)

Discovering Science: Matter, Rebecca Hunter (Raintree, 2003)

Using the Internet

Try searching the Internet to find out about silk. Websites can change, so if some of the links below no longer work, don't worry. Use a search engine such as www.yahooligans.com or www.internet4kids.com. You could try searching using the keywords 'silk farm', 'silk route' and 'silk trade'. Here are some websites to get you started.

Websites

A great site, which explains all about different materials:
http://www.bbc.co.uk/schools/revisewise/science/materials/

Find out more about the properties of different materials:
http://www.strangematterexhibit.com

Glossary

absorb soak up liquid

artificial made by man, rather than being made naturally

chemical substance that we use to make other substances or for jobs such as cleaning

cocoon case spun by a caterpillar

denier measure of how thick a fibre is

dye liquid added to something to change its colour

elastic able to recover its shape after being stretched

embroidery design that has been sewn on to something

environment world around us

fabric flat, bendy piece of material made from woven fibres

filament very fine strand

hatch emerge from an egg

incubator machine that keeps eggs warm

loom equipment on which fabric is woven

luxury something that is very comfortable and expensive but not necessary

merchant person who buys and sells goods

microscope instrument used for looking closely at things

mulberry type of tree originally from western Asia

mule animal whose father is a donkey and whose mother is a horse

natural anything that is not made by people

property characteristic or quality of a material

shuttle tool that carries thread across a loom

silk-screen printing way of printing pictures and designs

species group of living things that have certain features in common

spinnerets parts of an animal that spin silk

synthetic man-made

thermal insulator material that does not let heat pass through it

vat large container for liquids

warp threads vertical threads on a loom

waterproof material that does not let water pass through it

weft threads horizontal threads on a loom

Index

Titles in the *Using Materials* series include:

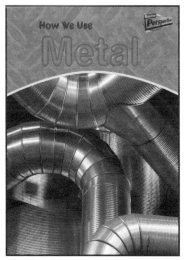

Hardback   1 844 43436 2

Hardback   1 844 43437 0

Hardback   1 844 43438 9

Hardback   1 844 43439 7

Hardback   1 844 43440 0

Hardback   1 844 43441 9

Find out about the other titles in this series on our website www.raintreepublishers.co.uk